# Self-Custody Of Digital Value

## By Crypto Thug

# INTRODUCTION

*"I've developed a new open-source P2P e-cash system called Bitcoin. It's completely decentralized, with no central server or trusted parties, because everything is based on crypto proof instead of trust. Give it a try, or take a look at the screen shots or design paper."*

*- The very first two sentences that Satoshi Nakamoto, the anonymous creator of Bitcoin, ever wrote on P2P Foundation, an early internet forum.*

The first time I purchased bitcoin, it was under $10. I bought a punk rock album from the website of a friend I no longer know. It took one and a half days from the night of his performance in Harrison, New Jersey, to learning to purchase bitcoin and setting up a wallet with private keys. I remember his album could only be purchased with bitcoin. His album was worth twenty dollars and I recall needing to purchase at least 9 Bitcoin to afford it. Later that year I lost my private keys. Several years later I lost the entire laptop. They say the best way to get serious about something is to take a loss and then bounce back. This is accurate advice because a loss can humble you and force you to examine what went wrong and where your values truly lie.

I'm proud to say I was converted by a true believer in Bitcoin long before it became popular. I was committed to showing my support for his art even though I had mixed feelings about punk rock music. It was his earnest and free-thinking nature that won me over. I remember him on stage after the show announcing that his album could only be purchased online with bitcoin. He helped me set up my first wallet by emailing me additional instructions. Now, I can say that he certainly changed my life.

I would rather not subject anyone to opening remarks on the virtue of limiting currency supply, difficulty rate adjustments, or complex mathematics. The common person hardly understands how money works. By the time you have finished this book you will know the difference between crypto currency and fiat currency and you will share an understanding of what "Self-Custody of Digital Value" could mean for everyone.

I elected to use the pseudonym 'Crypto Thug' as an homage to Satoshi Nakamoto as well as my old friend wherever he may be today. I am a known author. I have published several books on a variety of topics within the United States. None of my books have been about crypto currency. Over the years I came to understand that while many have a fantastic understanding of crypto currency there are very few who articulate it plainly with the common tongue. That is the mission of this book.

# Crypto Thug

Business Email: CryptoThug99@protonmail.com.

*"Bitcoin is a form of digital currency that can be used to buy and sell goods and services online. It is different from traditional currencies because it is not controlled by governments or banks. Instead, people use it directly between each other without needing traditional finance institutions. Bitcoin is quicker than most traditional payment methods and is becoming increasingly popular."*

- Chat GPT when asked, "Explain Bitcoin to an 80-year-old Boomer"

# Self-Custody Of Digital Value

I believe bitcoin to be the most significant economic invention in human history. This is because bitcoin provides us opportunity for self-custody of digital value. The ability for any individual to become a bank on the internet, to become the sole authority over where their digital value stays or goes, allows individuals to build capital free from legal, geopolitical, or third-party concerns. The unfettered opportunity to build capital via the self-custody of digital value is an incredible and historic achievement.

If Bitcoin were a company and you could purchase shares of this company, its product or service would be the opportunity to have self-custody of digital value for all individuals who understand how to use the internet as well as a crypto currency wallet. As an investor, you would then ask yourself 'How valuable will this service be in the future?' and 'Will people in the future be more or less willing to learn how to self-custody their digital value?'

In the past two years the government of Canada effectively shut down the bank accounts of peaceful covid policy protestors[1]. Not only did the government do that, they were allowed to freeze the bank accounts of all who donated to these peaceful protestors. The Canadian government, with help from the United States government, went so far as to freeze funds being sent through crowd funding websites. In other words, the government told the banks what to do and they complied. Imagine you are a shrewd investor, gazing out the window of your corner office at night pondering a future replete with third party government financial censorship. Will it be a future where governments can issue a hold on your bank accounts, freeze your stock portfolio, or 'reclassify' your real estate assets simply for speaking out of turn, protesting rather than complying, or not taking state sponsored medicines? Or will we embrace a type of technology that can free us from this centralized authoritarian nightmare? Will it be a future where individuals are embracing the use of crypto currency wallets, protecting their private keys, and assuming greater financial responsibility out of necessity?

In February of 2022, an Ontario Court issued an order to nine software companies demanding a disclosure of digital asset information

---

[1] "Trudeau vows to freeze anti mandate protesters' bank accounts, BBC, February 15th 2022, https://www.bbc.com/news/world-us-canada-60383385

and a freeze on all crypto currency wallets associated with the anti-vaccine protests that were occurring at the time[2]. These companies were in the business of creating and providing the internet with free software that anyone is able to download to take advantage of the opportunity to self-custody their digital value. This software is called a crypto currency wallet. From the beginning of bitcoin to today, all crypto currency is stored on some type of crypto currency wallet. If you are going to send crypto currency to someone, both you and the other person must have an actual crypto currency wallet. Even the popular exchanges where most people purchase crypto currency, such as Coinbase, must have native crypto currency wallets where their customers crypto currency reserves are safely stored.

The distinguishing feature of this network of crypto currency wallets is that they rely on no outside authority or third party to transact. In spite of that they operate with a greater degree of scalability transparency, and security than their digital fiat-currency predecessor. Most crypto currency wallets are independently owned and operated. Thus, they are sovereign pockets of digital value. Therefore, it is no surprise that all nine of these software companies declined to aid the government. None of them have the ability to freeze assets because the system they work to support is not a third-party reliant system. One of these companies,
Nunchuk.io, delivered a famous response to the Ontario Court[3]:

"We do not collect any user identification information beyond email addresses. We also do not hold any keys...Therefore: We cannot 'freeze' our users' assets; We cannot 'prevent' them from being moved; We do not have knowledge of 'the existence, nature, value and location' of our users' assets. This is by design."

"Please look up how self-custody and private keys work...When the Canadian dollar becomes worthless, we will be here to serve you, too."

---

[2] Court extends rare order to freeze up to $20 million in crypto, cash donations to 'freedom convoy', CBC, February 28th 2022, https://www.cbc.ca/news/canada/ottawa/marevainjunction-order-extended-freedom-convoy-crypto-financial-donations-frozen-1.6366975
[3] Marvel Induction Issued Against Nunchuck, Coincodecap.com, February 23 2022, https:// coincodecap.com/mareva-injunction-issued-against-nunchuk

*If you ask me that sounds like a crypto thug response.*

A government asking a crypto currency software provider to disclose the private keys of any crypto currency wallet is like a government asking 'MasterLock' to provide it with all five-digit combinations for their combination locks.  That is, until the government realizes it is the customers of Master Lock *themselves* who set their own unique five-digit combination. In fact, if there were anyone on Earth able to hack into a crypto currency wallet without using its own set of private keys, the reward in lost bitcoin would be billions upon billions of dollars. Lost bitcoin refers to the bitcoin that still exists on the network of wallets, however its owners have either lost their private keys or died without sharing them with another person.  Thus, the lost bitcoin are permanent islands of untouchable wealth, a strong reminder of how secure the technology is, and an even stronger reminder of how important it is that you do not give away or lose your private keys.

## SELF CUSTODY AND PRIVATE KEYS

When using the term "Self-Custody" the reference is to an asset you own or control that can only be taken from you via the use of physical force.  For example, the cash you keep in your safe is yours until someone points a gun to your head and asks for the combination to the safe or they forcibly remove the entire safe from your possession. The same is true for jewelry, art, collectibles, precious metals, and the private keys for crypto currency wallets. This category of assets can only be taken by use of physical force.  This is not true for real estate, stocks, bonds, businesses, patents, data or intellectual property. These assets can be taken by legal or political means as well as by force.

There are several types of crypto currency wallets and there are several types of private keys.  However, the purpose of this book is to help the beginner understand the overall value proposition of bitcoin and its related technologies. Therefore, the following is a simplified explanation of how private keys work.

In order to create a crypto currency wallet, you will first need to download the wallet either onto your phone, tablet, or computer. There are many 'brands' of wallets like there are many brands of bottled water. However, at the end of the day any real crypto currency wallet must contain is a unique set of private keys. Unique private keys, as well as a list of unique crypto currency addresses, are the distinguishing features of a crypto currency wallet in the same way water is the distinguishing feature of branded bottled water. Trust Wallet, Exodus Wallet, and Atomic Wallet are very popular 'brands' of crypto currency wallets that can be downloaded from the App Store. These and other wallets can also be downloaded on their respective websites.

After you download a crypto currency wallet, the first prompt you will be given will be a choice. Either you may "Create a new wallet" or "Restore an existing wallet".

Let us suppose you elect to create a new wallet. After you do so, you will be shown a unique set of 12 words. These are your private keys. Sometimes they are referred to as "seed phrases". Nobody else can view or access your 12-word seed phrases. That means that unless you give away your private keys, only you have the power to determine what coins will stay or leave your crypto currency wallet at any given moment. Think of it like owning the keys to a truck. Without them, you're not going to be able to use that truck.

Now it is time for a thought experiment. Let's suppose you meet someone very wealthy who wishes to pay you ten thousand in bitcoin and ten thousand dollar's worth of stable coins[4]. What do you do? The goal here is to transfer these digital currencies from their wallet to your wallet. In order for this to happen, the sender will need the "address" of the receiver, just like an email or a certified letter. Since the sender wishes to send two types of crypto currency, they will need two addresses: your new wallets bitcoin address and your new wallets stable coin address. Recall that a new wallet contains one unique address for each type of crypto currency that it supports. Therefore, you will provide the wealthy individual with your bitcoin address as well as your stable coin address. That individual will then be able to send both forms of crypto currency from his wallet addresses over to your wallet addresses. This will require two separate transactions. Each transaction can be viewed as one crypto currency address sending coins to another 'receiver' address.

Let us suppose that this wealthy individual has successfully sent you these two forms of crypto currency, wallet to wallet, and address to address. Your wallet now contains ten thousand in bitcoin and ten thousand in a stable coin. You now have control over where these funds can go because you are the only user utilizing the private keys that are associated with these two crypto currency addresses. As long as you have these private keys written down, you can throw your phone into the

---

[4] A stable coin is a category of crypto currency that is programmed to stay priced at exactly $1

ocean, download any "brand" of wallet you want, select "restore existing wallet", type your seed phrases into the text box, and lo and behold you will once again have access to the same addresses with the same funds. In other words, the value of your wallet is tied to the words of your seed phrases, not the brand of wallet that you download. You could download five different crypto currency wallets and type in the same set of seed phrases into each wallet. You will end up with five different ways to access the same exact set of funds. In other words, you will have five different apps on your phone and all of them will allow you to access the same wallet with its singular private keys, addresses, and funds.

Very often beginners in the crypto currency world will attempt to hide their address from public view because they mistakenly believe that this address will reflect some personal or private information, much like a physical address or an email address. This is not true. There is a limited amount of data that can be gleaned from knowing someone else's crypto currency address. In fact, it is possible for one person to create thousands of anonymous addresses in just one day. It is your seed phrases, not your crypto currency addresses, that are meant to be kept private. That is because seed phrases are the keys to controlling your crypto while addresses are merely used to identify where you want crypto currency to be sent. Nobody has the ability to steal your crypto currency using only a simple address.

Not too long ago someone asked me to send them a small amount of Ethereum. I told them that I would need their Ethereum address. Like many who dabble in crypto currency they acted as if they understood my request. Five minutes later I receive a photo (not a screen shot) of a piece of napkin covering the qr code address on their phone. I called to ask them,

"Please move the napkin so I can send you some Ethereum."

"How do I know you're not going to take my Ethereum?" they reply.

I tried an email analogy.

"If I need to email you, I need your email address?

It's the same here.

"Then why does it say $2400?"

"That's the price of Ethereum."

It is moments like these that brought me to writing this book. It has been weeks since this conversation. I am still waiting for that Ethereum address. There is much more to crypto beyond buying and selling it on Coinbase. Yet as is so often the case in finance, it is the people that know nothing who are truly never in doubt.

## DODGING SCAMMERS

Since its already the second chapter let's discuss how to stay safe out there in the digital wild west that is crypto currency before you put down this book and end up handing your life savings over to a North Korean Chat Bot pretending to be Craig from Coinbase customer service.

Rule Number One: Never give away your private keys. Coinbase will never ask you for them. Nobody presenting to help you will ever need them for any reason whatsoever. Also do not upload your raw set of private keys to the cloud. There have been several incidences of people hacking into clouds and commandeering other people's keys.

Rule Number Two: When in doubt do nothing and stay tight. Most crypto currency scams require you to make the first move. Very often that first move requires getting you to connect your wallet to their website. Be certain of which wallets you decide to connect to any website. I would recommend exploring the crypto currency multiverse with a wallet that contains minimal value.

Another popular way to get you to make the first move is to send you some "funny money" If suddenly ten million dollar's worth of an anomalous cryptocurrency just happens to show up in your wallet one day do not attempt to send it anywhere because in doing so, you may incur a tremendous fee that is paid to the criminal who sent you the funny money in the first place.

Rule Number Three: Use two-factor authentication. This rule, is actually rule number one for how to browse the web securely, in general. You really do remove a significant amount of risk when you use two factor authentication.

Rule Number Four: Use cryptography in real life. You will have to hide your 12-word seed phrases. The more sophisticated your method of hiding, the more you secure the bag. Crypto currency is a throwback to the days of cryptography when people sent letters and wrote books with hidden encrypted messages in them. Believe it or not this was extremely popular for a very long time among literate people of the world.

Let us suppose a certain author were to write a book in order to help his peers understand the practical basics of crypto currency. Within that book they hid their own twelve-word seed phrase. It might be the 16th and 32nd word of the first six chapters. That author would be hiding their money in plain sight, yet only they would know what words to search for within the hypothetical crypto currency book. You can get creative with this rule.

## DIGITAL SCARCITY

Congratulations, you have made it all the way to Chapter three without committing a federal crime. Try to imagine a world in which five business partners, each living in a different country, have access to the same crypto currency wallet that they use for their business. All five partners are equal partners in this venture and therefore they share the same set of private keys. In spite of the fact that one may live in Malaysia and another in Hawaii they are able to draw upon the same set of resources. None of these business partners will ever need to send money to the other. Take a minute to think about what this could mean for the international money changers, the central banks.

Central banks have a threefold manifesto. First, they are involved in setting international prices in the commodities markets. Second, they control the exchange of international currency and they make a pretty penny from doing that. Third, they control interest rates which inevitably determine the rates at which they print money out of thin air. "Out of thin air" is a colloquialism. In actuality over 97% of the money in the world is digital. That money is literally a text file on a computer. It is not backed by a quantifiable substance or even a quantifiable idea. It is often posited that military force is what backs the global dollar and that the United States would "Police the Worlds Ocean" in exchange for total dominion over the life blood of a world economy, its currency. Still, it is no wonder why the government tends to hoard gold in places like fort Knox. At the end of the day, you cannot fill your coffers with military force. It cannot be measured or weighed. It is only an idea.

There is a person on this planet that gets paid to perform the task of creating one million dollars and they do this with seven easy clicks of their space bar. You may find it hard to believe that most government expenditure does not come from tax money. It is true. Most government expenditure is from money the fed creates when our government provides bonds to the federal reserve in exchange for debt. After our government gives these bonds to the federal reserve the fed will create money, in a text file, send it to the government with a notice to pay back their loan at some point in the future. In other words, nearly 31 trillion dollars of "national debt" was originally created in a text file on a central bank computer. Therefore, in order to remove that debt, you simply dispose of the computer.

Now let's return to our five business partners. Notice how they are skirting around the international financial system. They have no need to sell their own national currency to the money changers or wait several days for the notoriously expensive SWIFT system to complete their transaction after their personal data has been tracked and logged. They have no need to send money to each other at all because they all pour their water from the same well. Likewise, they all work to replenish the same well. Since their source of capital is beyond the reach of central banks or third parties, any local businesses that once followed international pricing rules now has the opportunity to skirt this unenforceable, censorious regulation.

Satoshi Nakamoto, the anonymous creator of Bitcoin, once wrote "The root problem with conventional currencies is all the trust that's required to make it work". Satoshi Nakamoto also left a message inside of the original "genesis" block of the bitcoin public ledger. It reads 'The Times 03/Jan/2009 Chancellor on brink of second bailout for banks. Clearly, central bank quantitative easing was an issue Satoshi Nakamoto was eager to resolve.

In presenting Bitcoin, Satoshi Nakamoto also brought the world another entirely novel achievement: Digital Scarcity.

The internet, as most people still know it today, contains an incredible amount of value. Most of this value is in the inherent democratization of information that it provides us. However, nothing on the internet, itself contains any tangible value. You cannot pay someone in emails or web pages because this digital infrastructure can be easily copied, easily altered, and shared forever. There are no scarce materials within the internet like there are scarce materials within Earth. That is because everything on the internet can be copied ad infinitum.

The actual physical universe itself behaves very differently. It is based on an infinite variety model. No snowflake is ever alike. A single gust of wind is unique. The leaf that you pluck from a tree is unique. Once you crumple that leaf in your hand, it exists nowhere else in the universe. A single leaf from a tree cannot be copied like the text from your favorite websites.

Most people still believe the internet is a place where scarcity does not exist, a place where anything can be copied. This is no longer true. There is something that can now exist in exactly one place on the internet and only that place. If it moves, it is no longer there, because it has moved to a new location. Like the leaf it cannot be copied, saved to a cloud, or altered in any way. That something mimicking the natural laws of the physical universe is bitcoin.

If you send bitcoin to an address, it will only exist at that address. It will not be copied or saved in a "sent" folder like an email. It will only exist at that address. Therefore, the currency cannot be debased because it exists within a secure system that exhibits the qualities of natural scarcity. This 'Digital Scarcity' is the true miracle behind the technology that empowers bitcoin. In order to achieve this feat of computer science, Satoshi Nakamoto created an algorithm that provided a solution to what is known as the Byzantine Generals problem. To do this Nakamoto created what is known the Nakamoto Consensus Algorithm[5]. Currently this algorithm is considered a breakthrough and is now included within the computer science curriculum of several top universities.

How about another example of digital scarcity? Imagine it is 2045 and you are in your car about to be pulled over by the police. When they approach the window, they ask for your driver's license. You pull out your phone and open the exclusive DMV app. The Police scan your driver's license to verify its authenticity. The scanner checks with the DMV blockchain database to make sure your driver's license is not a copy or altered in any way. That is because your driver's license is protected by digital scarcity. How is this? Because your driver's license is now an NFT. This NFT behaves like a bitcoin. It can only be in one place at one time and it obeys the laws of digital scarcity. Your driver's license NFT is currently registered with you. The police verify this, then give you a warning, and you are free to go. This is just one of potentially millions of use cases for digital scarcity.

## WHAT IS SCARCITY?

---

[5] Nakamoto Consensus Algorithm:  It is **a Byzantine fault tolerant consensus algorithm that works in conjunction with proof of work (PoW) to govern the Bitcoin blockchain**. Byzantine fault tolerance (BFT) is a condition where a distributed system can remain faulttolerant in the presence of malicious actors and network imperfection

At the beginning of the second chapter of this book we discussed what "Self-Custody" means. 'Self-Custody' refers to a class of assets that can only be taken by physical force. Recall that 'Self Custody of Digital Value' is the primary product or service of this blockchain currency experiment known as Bitcoin. Now let's discuss the word "Value".

To put it simply, value exists at the intersection of scarcity and necessity. Great need matched with great scarcity will always produce great value. For example, everyone needs air. Air is an immutable necessity. Yet air is free because its supply is seemingly infinite. Clean drinking water is another matter. Water is an immutable necessity. The supply of clean potable water in the world is slowly diminishing, however. Therefore, the value of water must slowly rise. You are able to track the value of an asset by its price.

Prices are not meant to be fixed. They are meant to change. A change in price indicates a change in how society values something. Let's assume tomorrow that the price of silver sharply falls. Perhaps this means the supply of silver has expanded? Perhaps it means the markets that use silver have found a superior product? There must be a reason for the changing price of silver. This reason is found either on the demand side or the supply side of the equation.

A shrewd investor always wants to know why the prices of things change. Unusual price activity is often the first clue that leads a researcher or investor to discover possible trends or other ways to make money. The more unadulterated prices are in any given market, the more transparent that market is to the investor. If you have a transparent market, you are able to better predict future necessity and address it, leading to progress. However, if you set prices by law or mandate you greatly impede the market-based resolution of future necessity.

Within any market the value of any asset will depend on both the state of demand and supply for that asset. This is true for stocks, real estate, bonds, and yes, also bitcoin. Scarcity directly impacts the supply side of any market. Scarcity indirectly effects the demand side of any market as well. Likewise, necessity directly effects the demand side of market. It also indirectly effects the supply side. Scarcity and necessity are the respective epitomes of supply and demand. This may sound so important that it should be taught in school. It is not.

If you were to google "The price of bitcoin is determined by its…" you will be told:

"The *price* of bitcoin is determined in the same way that the *value* of the US dollar is determined: Supply and Demand."


The price of bitcoin is not determined by law or mandate. It is a pure supply and demand model. The supply side of Bitcoin is entirely preprogrammed, limited, and immutable. The demand side of Bitcoin is determined by its value. Value exists at the intersection of scarcity and necessity.

The price of the dollar on the other hand is determined by an "impure" supply and demand model wherein important prices and wages are periodically set by mandate while total supply and rate of supply are dominated by the whims of an elite financial class[6]. In other words, bitcoin represents a pure capitalist meritocracy while the dollar and the world economy represent a corrupt hybrid socialist/capitalist meritocracy. This is why old Austrian economists have always been popular among the bitcoin community. Bitcoin is more closely aligned with the original ideas of capital theory or capitalism as espoused by the likes of F.A. Hayek, Ludwig von Mises, and Carl Menger. In fact, Nobel Prize winning economist F.A. Hayek once spoke directly to the need for Bitcoin in an interview from 1984: "I don't believe we shall ever have a good money again before we take the thing out of the hands of the government. We cannot take it violently out of the hands of the government. All we can do, in some sly or roundabout way, is introduce something they can't stop."[7]

You may have noticed that google did not lie to you. It used the words value and price rather appropriately. The search engines answer is nonetheless deceptive. Yes, the value of literally *anything* is determined by its supply and demand equation. Every product or service ever created was priced within a supply and demand framework. However, we can only arrive at a pricing *method* when conditions within the supply and demand equation have been accounted for and then integrated. The price of bitcoin is determined by its value as well as predetermined computer code. The price of the dollar is determined,

---

[6] The financial class can either create money out of thin air or call for loans to be repaid. Since all fiat value is interpreted as debt/loans they have the ability to expand capital markets or drain them at will. This is how they control the supply side of the global market.

[7] https://news.bitcoin.com/hayeks-1984-rediscovered-footage-shows-austrian-economistpredicting-bitcoin/

day by day, by its value and the decisions of various people. These pricing methods are not the same.

Imagine asking google, "How did Michael Jordan win six championships?" and receiving this response:

"Michael Jordan and his team were able to 'get the ball through the basket.'"

You then ask, "Why was Kobe Bryant so good at passing the ball?"

"Kobe Bryant was able to help 'get the ball through the basket'"

This is like answering every important economics question with the short phrase: 'Its Supply and Demand'.

## FALSE SCARCITY, FALSE NECESSITY

The only way to control a society is by injecting a controllable amount of false scarcity and false necessity into that society. It is well known that Europeans used glass beads as a form of currency with which they bought Africa. Glass beads were easy to produce in Europe while relatively unknown in Africa. The people there were assaulted with a formidable intellectual weapon, false scarcity.

Similarly, we are being assaulted with weapons of false necessity. We are told we need to pay taxes while the government and the fed type most of their yearly expenditure into a glorified text file. We are told we need medicines that later do not appear to work. We are told our money needs to be backed by something when in fact it does not have to be backed by anything tangible, rather it must serve as a trusted meta property with great salability through time and space. In other words, the ideal money is one which never deteriorates or degrades and must be able to be sent in very large or small amounts, to anywhere in the world, in a moment.

This is why I believe bitcoin to be the most significant economic invention ever created. It was designed to be a civilizational check against false scarcity.

# SELF CUSTODY OF DIGITAL VALUE

In order to seize property from regular folks, without their consent, the government employs what is known as eminent domain. Eminent domain is the area law that is designed to take land and property away from you. If you are interested in preserving your real estate you can begin investigating land patents. This may not help you against eminent domain, however.

In order to seize your stocks, your brokerage must receive what is known as a money judgement. This is essentially notice of a debt that is backed by the weight of the United States government. A small number of brokerages are immune to garnishments by way of money judgements, however.

There are a number of ways our government can seize your business. If it is large enough to be a publicly traded company, the government can purchase the majority of equity in the company and thus nationalize the business. Primarily this has been done in media, banking, fossil fuels, telecommunications, railways, airlines, post offices, and the water industries. Most people do not realize that airlines are a nationalized industry.

Another way that government can seize your business is if the federal reserve raises rates to the point where irresponsible small banks begin to fail. Once those banks fail, its business customers will be bankrupt and their assets might be purchased at discounted rates.

In 1949, the government authorized itself to exercise eminent domain over patents.
This is title 28 of USC section 1498.

Obviously, if banks held 1:1 reserves for their customers there would hardly be reason for a bank insolvency. However, we do not live in that type of world and banks are simply allowed to gamble with your money. "Fractional Reserve Banking" is what it implies, banks are allowed to hold a fraction of their reserve to customer funds. They take the rest of your money and gamble it. To date the top three bank insolvencies in the United States have been Washington mutual at approximately 300 billion in assets, Silicon Valley bank at approximately 200 billion, and Signature bank at approximately 110 billion. The latter two insolvencies occurred in 2023.

President Roosevelt and the gold seizure act of 1933 were rather effective at removing the gold from the population and delivering to the United States treasury, where it would later be hypothecated away to another market. In 1974 president Ford once again legalized private ownership of gold coins bars and certificates.

The forty-year banning gold is what allowed our fiat currency to take prominence. Fiat means, "by formal decree". Our fiat currency is backed by our governments "formal decree". It is not currently backed by gold. The federal reserve and our government control the growth rate of our total supply of dollars. Over 97% of global dollars are online and digital. According to Elon Musk, cofounder of PayPal, "Money is essentially and online database...The money system, for practical purposes, is really just a bunch of heterogeneous mainframes running old Cobol, literally in batch mode. I pity the poor bastard that has to maintain that code[8]" Cobol (common business-oriented language) code first appeared in 1959. Bitcoin was first launched in 2009. Bitcoin uses C++ programming, which was invented in 1983 and first appearing in 1997.

These old Cobol mainframes are literally the plumbing of the global financial system. Currently over 40% of banks and 95% of bank ATM's operate using Cobol. The individuals who control these Cobol mainframes have "editing privileges". Nevertheless, if a significant amount of these centralized Cobol mainframes are damaged the entire financial system will be at risk. That is why they are protected. The difference between digital fiat and Bitcoin essentially highlights the difference between the centralized Cobol mainframes and the decentralized global network of Bitcoin miners.

The decentralized nature of bitcoin miners provides the network with a "hydra" advantage. In order to get rid of bitcoin you have to destroy every single miner in the world. Whether it is connected to the internet or not does not matter. Whether the power goes out globally does not matter. The network can go dormant and restart. Even if there were just one miner working, perhaps from a remote Siberian holdout with decent internet connection, the bitcoin network will be up and running. Like the saying goes, "Cut the head off one and two will grow back". That is the core advantage of being decentralized like the bitcoin network.

---

[8] Episode 252, 'The Lex Friedman Podcast' featuring Elon Musk

From the feds financial "editing privileges" to the homestead act of 1862, to people pretending to be Elon Musk asking you to send them any amount of Bitcoin in order for them "send back double that amount", people tend to steal and horde other peoples accumulated value in ever more creative ways. Likewise, there is an ever-changing premium on the assurances of self-custody. If you increase someone's incentive to accumulate value in the long term, they will be able to execute long term decisions.

## SILVER & GOLD

There were two advantages of gold as a global reserve for currency. First, gold has salability over time. Gold cannot oxidize or rust like other metals. Gold does not degrade over the long term. Thus, it can be inherited through generations of people. Silver possesses the same advantage. However, for most of human history it was extraordinarily difficult to *increase the annual rate of new gold supply*. That means that most of the gold reserves in this world were actually mined centuries years ago. The reason it was difficult to increase the annual rate of new gold supply was because gold itself has historically been very difficult to mine. This resulted in supply stability.

On March 27th, 1980, Nelson, William, and Lamar Hunt attempted to corner the silver market by hoarding a very large amount of silver. As they stockpiled silver, they placed large bets on silver in the futures markets and very soon after the price of silver spiked. This event became known as "Silver Thursday".

What the hunt brothers did not expect was that this substantial investment in silver allowed the silver miners to turn around and increase the annual rate of new silver supply by almost twenty percent! Thus, the price of silver fell from its peak of $25 to $16 that same year. A flexible annual rate of increase is not good for supply stability.

A similar event could not have taken place within the gold market. If gold miners were handed billions of dollars through large sales, a reinvestment into mining would not yield a 20% increase in gold supply for the year. A substantial investment into gold mining would have yielded at most a .3%-1.5% increase for the year.

Now you can see another reason why the Chinese and Indian Empires, whose economies were backed by silver, fell to the British

Empire which relied on the gold standard. After one generation silver became oversupplied, ruining the economies of both China and India. This is a very valuable lesson to those who truly study economic warfare and history.

It is also easier to see why having a predictable supply curve through time can increase adoption of a currency standard, as is the case with Bitcoin and gold.

Please note that within the last fifty years the technology for mining gold has exponentially improved. Moreover, it is widely believed that the gold market has been diluted with "paper gold". In other words, there are more certificates promising to be backed by gold than there is actually gold held in reserve. Gold used to be a sensible reserve standard. Things have changed, however.

## CASHING OUT & EXCHANGES

It is very likely that you or someone you know have purchased crypto currency on an exchange. Some of the most popular exchanges today are Binance, Coinbase, Kucoin, and Gemini. These corporate exchanges allow the average person to create their own account, similar to a stock exchange. These exchange accounts are often mistaken for true crypto currency wallets[9]. Your account with these exchanges does provide you with a unique list of crypto currency addresses, yet do not provide you with their associated private keys.

That is why it is best to use exchanges as an on ramp or off ramp for the exchange of crypto currency and digital fiat currency. If you are looking to sell your crypto currency or cash out you may use these exchanges. Similarly, if you are looking to purchase crypto currency and self-custody that digital value, you may begin by purchasing some on an exchange and then send it to a wallet of your own. Since these exchanges provide you with one address per crypto currency, you are able to send crypto currency to that address in order to sell it or send it from that address when you are ready to remove your crypto currency from the hands of a profit driven corporation.

---

[9] Coinbase and Kucoin also offer their own brands of crypto currency wallet called 'The Coinbase wallet' and 'KuCoin Wallet'. These are actual crypto currency wallets, not exchange accounts. This is often is a source of confusion.

Historically exchanges have been riddled with problems and it is not wise to leave your digital value exposed on an exchange where it can be subject to seizure via corporate bankruptcy or potentially non blockchain related hacks.

If you are nervous about sending or receiving bitcoin or other crypto currency for the first time a great cardinal rule to follow is to send small amounts, or test amounts, before sending or receiving larger amounts that make you feel less comfortable. Remember this technology allows you to send millions of dollar's worth of value around the world in three seconds without a trusted third party. However, if you send it to the wrong address or expose your private keys to someone else, that one is on you. If you are a beginner you should get in the habit of sending test amounts from wallet to wallet. There is an emotional learning involved in the self-custody your own value.

There are other ways to sell or purchase crypto currency. You can purchase property, goods, or services on the open market with crypto currency and then sell them at a later date. You can also send crypto currency to a willing participant, wallet to wallet, in exchange for cash. In these instances, stable coins are often used to hold the exact value of the transaction for both parties. You may also use a bitcoin ATM. If you do elect to use a bitcoin or crypto currency ATM, make sure it is able to receive crypto currency and provide you with cash. Many bitcoin ATMs only offer users the opportunity purchase and send crypto currency elsewhere. In countries like Nigeria, you can send your crypto to a business that will hold it as collateral and they will issue you a digital or paper fiat loan based on that crypto currency collateral.
Collateral based loans and other traditional financial services are available in a new
'blockchain' version called "Defi."

## WHAT IS DECENTRALIZED FINANCE?

Please remember to never connect your cryptocurrency wallet to any website unless you trust that website. The decentralized finance world is replete with scams. However, the most promising innovations are also occurring within the realm of 'Defi'. These promising innovations include decentralized exchanges, non-fungible tokens or NFT's, and collateral based loans. Other riskier areas of decentralized finance that may be of interest include staking and decentralized insurance.

A decentralized exchange (DEX) provides crypto wallet users with the ability to trade or "swap" their coins, for a fee, and usually from within the wallet itself. Unlike centralized exchanges, a DEX does not rely on any third party to transact. A portion of trading fees are paid to those who elect to hold a substantial amount of their capital on these decentralized exchanges. This system incentivizes crypto holders to share a percentage of their funds with the DEX and it in turn allows the DEX enough capital to supply any trades.

Non fungible tokens (NFTs) are tokens that cannot be traded equivalently with other assets. In other words, it allows for tokenization of assets like sports contracts, franchise ownership, art or even real estate. Tokenization means it is possible to take such an asset and split it into a number of "pieces" so that they can be collectively owned.

Spencer Dinwiddie, point guard for the Brooklyn nets and self-described "tech guy with a jumper" tokenized his 34-million-dollar contract with the Brooklyn nets. They were sold as security tokens. He received much of his three-year salary up front. Investors in his contract were paid back their principle as well as dividends.

A collateral based system of loans would seem to be the sensible way to do things. After all, if you have one hundred dollars and you give it to a bank then that bank would be happy to loan you up to fifty dollars because they have a guarantee that if you do not pay back your loan, they will simply deduct fifty dollars from your collateral deposit. Strangely, this is not how loans work in traditional finance. Banks are allowed to make loans while holding only a fraction of the loan amount itself. However, users of DEFI have access to automated, non-third-party collateralized loans.

Across the majority DEFI platforms users are encouraged to vote on changes or upgrades to their respective projects. That is because most of the services within DEFI operate as DAO's or *decentralized autonomous organizations*. That means there are no CEOs or board of executives governing the actions of these new financial services tools.

## TRILEMMA PLUS TOOLS OF THE TRADE

What makes bitcoin different from other coins? There are several ways to compare the 'OG' with its children. The Bitcoin network can calculate quintillions of hashes every second. One quintillion is a million million millions (try saying that fast three times). Bitcoin is the most powerful computing network that exists on the internet. It is also the most powerful collection of processing power ever created. This is because bitcoin runs on what is known as "Proof of work". Proof of work basically means a bunch of bitcoin miners are holding up the most powerful computer network in the world by doing actual work. That work is immense calculative computing power and requires significantly more electrical energy than the most common alternative, "Proof of Stake". This calculative computing power is what maintains the incredible security of the Bitcoin network. This calculative computing power is what literally "backs" Bitcoin, if you care to consider it that way. Bitcoin is not the only proof work coin. Monero is another fine example of a proof of work decentralized computing network. Like Bitcoin, Monero never had an 'Initial Coin Offering'[10]. Many of its important contributors are still unknown and often long-time veterans of the internet. Monero is similar to bitcoin in many ways however it is a privacy enhanced network. Monero is the most privacy secured currency in the world.

Proof of stake basically means a select group will stake their share of coins within the network, leaving them there to allow for greater security scalability and decentralization. Proof of stake seeks to achieve the same result as proof of work yet by different means. Both proof of stake networks and proof of work networks seek to optimize what is known as the Trilemma: security, scalability, and decentralization. Usually in order to function successfully, programmers of new crypto currencies will have to make tradeoffs between the three options. Projects that appear promising have usually solved the trilemma to some greater degree than others.

For example, Visa can process transactions at a rate of 1700 per second. Solana, a cryptocurrency, can process 65,000 transactions per second and has been able to handle over 100,000 tps for a long periods of time. Transactions per second is a measure of speed which falls under the category of scalability. The bitcoin network is slower, processing about 20 transactions per second. However, where Bitcoin lacks in speed and scalability it makes up for in security and decentralization.

The Trilemma is an excellent framework for evaluating crypto currency projects. Another way to compare Bitcoin with other coins is through the Howie test. The Howie test is a test to determine whether a transaction qualifies as a "investment contract" and is therefore a security. In order for something to be considered a security it must 1) Be

---

[10] An initial coin offering or ICO is a when an organization makes a first time offer of their token to the market, usually to help raise money. Early investors typically receive a premium on the token being offered.

an investment of money 2) In a common enterprise 3) with the expectation of profit 4) to be derived from the effort of others. Securities are regulated and taxed differently when compared to derivatives or commodities.

Both Bitcoin and Ethereum do not pass the Howie test and are not considered securities. However, many other coins could be considered securities and these coins happen to be built using the Ethereum network and other similar projects.

To begin evaluating crypto currency projects you will need an application on your phone or website that can allow you to view all crypto currency and their respective statistics in a user-friendly way. I recommend using CoinGecko or Coinmarketcap.com.

To evaluate a cryptocurrency public ledger you can visit their respective websites. For example. blockchain.com/explorer can help you search the entire Bitcoin public ledger. etherscan.io will allow you to search within the Ethereum network. bscscan.com will allow you to search the BNB network.  All you need to begin your search is a transaction ID or crypto currency address.

Another important tool to have in the crypto world are the communication/information applications: Telegram, discord, reddit, and medium. You will have to be very careful avoiding scams, once again. You will also find valuable information about upcoming relevant crypto currency projects and events using these tools.

Not too long ago a friend called me asking for help.  She told me she had been hacked and that the crypto currency in her wallet was missing.  Naturally, I asked if she shared her private keys with anyone. "Only Coinbase" was the answer she gave.

Believe it or not this sort of mistake is quite common. There is no universal manual for operating crypto currency, outside of this book of course.  I explained to my friend that unfortunately a hacker poising as Coinbase had compromised her funds.  This hacker promptly removed some Ethereum from their account.  However, what they did next turned out to be much more interesting.

The hacker noticed that a $500 sum of BNB (currently the world's third largest crypto currency) was locked.  In order to unlock it, a fee of $3 had to be paid in BNB.  The wallet did not have a sufficient amount of liquid BNB to use to pay the fee.  Therefore, the hacker had to send BNB to this newly hacked address. In doing so it exposed its BNB sender address because, as mentioned, the entire BNB network can be viewed transparently using bscscan.com. I would encourage you to look up this address yourself:


**bnb1xrfwzlu9c5208lhtn7ywt0mjrhjh4nt4fjyqxy**


You may use clank app, explorer BNB, Bscscan or any other provider to view the history of transactions associated with the above address.  This is excellent homework for someone intending to learn more about crypto currency. The first thing you will notice about this address is that it started out, a couple of years ago, with approximately 80 million dollars.

The next thing you probably realized is that it is sending out a very tiny amount of BNB almost every other minute. For several years this address has sent out small amounts of BNB every other minute. That is because this address is operated a robot.

My friend explained that she received a prompt on her computer from "what appeared to be Coinbase" requesting she type in her twelve-word seed phrase.  This prompt is part of a massive automated system of fraud and the robot operating the above address is an equally important part of that system.

When you introduce scarcity into any environment you are going to have crime.  It is true that crypto currency allows for monied criminal interests to hide their capital. Scarcity also creates new abilities to solve old forms of crime, however. Digital Scarcity already allows for far more accurate and reliable systems of voting and the preservation of the public record.  At the end of the day, if you follow the precautions mentioned in this book you will avoid most potential issues.


## STABLE COIN SHELVING


Stable coins have become increasingly controversial and popular. I would not recommend you put a large amount of value into stable coins unless you are confident in the long-term value of your chosen stable coin.  USDC, DAI, BUSD, USDT, and are among the most popular options to consider.

The money changers who own digital fiat have good reason to be anti-stable coin. Stable coins provide the people with a growing number of options to use other than a central bank digital currency. We all know a CBDC will be used to track trace and database the whole of society. That is why it is important to own and be familiar with stable coins. However, do not go overboard or hoard only one type of stable coin.

An excellent idea would be to take a modest percentage of your overall wealth and convert it into various stable coins. Next, create numerous wallets and keep the private keys to these wallets safely hidden. Send an equal amount of stable coins to each wallet. Now you quite literally have your dollar value secured through time and within numerous banks that you control. You are storing the value of your hard-earned dollars in a place no one can access other than you. This is called stable coin shelving. With these technologies and instructions, you can for the first time ever provide yourself the service that a bank would typically provide: custody of the digital dollar. This is an important milestone in finance however at present it is often overlooked. You are also ensuring that you do not keep all of your eggs in one basket by creating numerous wallets. In addition to that, you are not attracting any unwanted attention by only having one wallet with a potentially very large and attractive amount.

Perhaps this is why over 80% of all trades involve stable coins yet stable coins comprise less than 20% of the overall market cap[11] of the crypto currency Industry. It is very useful to capture the value of the digital dollar yet and yet rely on nobody other than yourself to custody them.

If you want to take stable coins shelving to the next level, purchase a smart phone that is capable of connecting to wifi. Make sure you do not have any pre-existing personal information on this phone. You do not need to purchase a phone number. Connect that phone to Wi-Fi and download a few crypto currency wallets from their respective websites. Write down your associated private keys for these digitally anonymous wallets. Then send stable coins to these wallets for stockpiling digital value. If you download exodus wallet you will be able to swap stable coins for monero, using its built in DEX. This is called the "burner phone" option.

---

[11] Market capital refers to the total dollar value invested into the project

## SCALABILITY INTEROPERABILITY & ADOPTION

If you are like most people, you probably would like to know which projects in crypto currency have any substantial long-term value. There will be no specific coin recommendations in this book other than bitcoin. However, it is clear that projects that focus on scalability, user adoption, and interoperability will inevitably win the day. This is because people prefer projects with decent network speed and require a range of optional financial services.

Interoperability is a primary trend among burgeoning crypto currency projects. For example, on the Ethereum network you are able to build entire online businesses. There is already a blockchain based "Airbnb of Ethereum" called 'DTravel'. There are also uber alternatives. These and other projects are able to create new tokens that are native to the Ethereum network. You read that correctly. Tokens can be created *within* tokens, so to speak. In fact, many of the top 100 coins by market cap were built on top of the Ethereum network.
These new businesses and their respective tokens could be considered securities, of course. However, the ground which they are able to thrive, Ethereum, functions as a resource for these securities and is therefore not a security.

The crypto currency economy will be built upon Bitcoin if it is to be built anywhere. However, it may also be built upon Ethereum, Cardano, Cosmos, Matic and other projects that emphasize scalability, interoperability, and new user adoption.

## FINAL THOUGHTS

At this moment in history, we are truly teetering on the brink of a central bank controlled digital currency and inching closer toward a tracked, traced, and controlled society. A fair and reasonable money system must be the first solution to such a profound spiritual threat to our civilization. We must not acquiesce. Do not accept the central bank digital currency. You have a stronger alternative in Bitcoin.

It is my hope that the information in this book has helped move you closer toward becoming financially sovereign.

A Special Thank You To All Those Who Helped Crypto Thug

www.ingramcontent.com/pod-product-compliance
Lightning Source LLC
Chambersburg PA
CBHW072228290526
45794CB00007B/2930